7 Steps Every First-Time Franchise Buyer Should Follow

Plus:
49 Insider Secrets
You Need to Know
&
3 Deadly Traps to Avoid

Mark C. Leonard

© 2014 by **Mark C. Leonard**

All Rights Reserved. No part of this publication may be reproduced in any form or by any means, including scanning, photocopying, or otherwise without prior written permission of the copyright holder.

First Printing, 2014

Printed in the United States of America

ISBN 978-1494868642

Income Disclaimer

This document contains business strategies, marketing methods and other business advice that, regardless of my own results and experience, may not produce the same results (or any results) for you. I make absolutely no guarantee, expressed or implied, that by following the advice below you will make any money or improve current profits, as there are several factors and variables that come into play regarding any given business.

Primarily, results will depend on the nature of the product or business model, the conditions of the marketplace, the experience of the individual, and situations and elements that are beyond your control.

As with any business endeavor, you assume all risk related to investment and money based on your own discretion and at your own potential expense.

Liability Disclaimer

By reading this document, you assume all risks associated with using the advice given below, with a full understanding that you, solely, are responsible for anything that may occur as a result of putting this information into action in any way, and regardless of your interpretation of the advice.

You further agree that our company cannot be held responsible in any way for the success or failure of your business as a result of the information presented below. It is your responsibility to conduct your own due diligence regarding the safe and successful operation of your business if you intend to apply any of our information in any way to your business operations.

Terms of Use

You are given a non-transferable, "personal use" license to this product. You cannot distribute it or share it with other individuals.

Also, there are no resale rights or private label rights granted when purchasing this document. In other words, it's for your own personal use only.

7 Steps Every First-Time Franchise Buyer Should Follow

Plus:
49 Insider Secrets
You Need to Know
&
3 Deadly Traps to Avoid

Table of Contents

Introduction 1

Step 1 - Suitability 5
    Your Personality 6
    Your Motivation 7
    Your Money Situation 8
    Other Franchisee Suitability 9
    Franchisor Suitability 10
    Area Developer Suitability 11
    Employee Suitability 13

Step 2 - Trends 15
    National Trends 15
    Local Trends 16
    Franchisor Trends 17
    Real Estate Trends 19
    Employment Trends 19
    Legal/Governmental Trends 20

Step 3 - Location 23
    New Locations 23
    Existing Locations 26
    Leases and Landlords 32
    Assignments: Landlord 37
    Assignments: Franchisor 39

Step 4 - Due Diligence 43
    Litigation 43
    Franchisee Obligations 44

Territory	45
Franchisee Research	46
Franchisee Relations	51
Franchisor Training and Inspections	51
Purchasing Methodology	52
Competition	53

Step 5 - Employees 55
Skill Sets Required 55
On-site or Absentee 57
Family 58
Family Upside 60
Workers Comp 61
Health Care 61
Sick-leave, PTO 63
Other Benefits 64
Wage Trends 64
Surveillance 65

Step 6 - Marketing/ Advertising 69
National Marketing funds 69
Local area funds 71
Store/Business marketing 71
Customer Service 74

Step 7 - Business Plan 77
Labor Schedule 77
Lease 78
Financing 80
Create a Mastermind Team 81
Selling the Business 82

The 3 Deadly Traps 83
Deadly Trap #1: "Franchises are safe" 83
Deadly Trap #2: "The Ideal Location" 84
Deadly Trap #3: "Business in a Box" 86

Conclusion 89

Appendix 1 - The 49 Secrets 91
    Step 1 - Suitability 91
    Step 2 - Trends 92
    Step 3 - Location 93
    Step 4 - Due Diligence 94
    Step 5 - Employees 95
    Step 6 - Marketing/Advertising 96
    Step 7 - Business Plan 97

Resources 98

About the Author 99

Introduction

By purchasing this book, you have taken a giant step in preparing for your future as an entrepreneur. If you are thinking about buying a franchise or small business, the idea of owning and running your own company is probably both intriguing and somewhat scary.

Let me warn you that this book is not intended to be an inspirational, "You Can Do It!" book. There are plenty of those available and many of them are useless. I am writing this for you based on my experience as a multi-unit owner of one of the most popular franchises in the world. This book comes from my experience, and those of many other franchisees who left the traditional job market and plunged into the world of owning a franchise.

This is what you need to know: becoming a franchisee can be as dangerous as it is rewarding and can lead to financial devastation, especially for the unwary.

My intention for writing this book is to provide you with the critical information I wish I had when I started investing in a franchise.

I learned the hard way. When you pay attention to the secrets and suggested actions contained in this book, you will be able to answer the following critical questions.

- Is buying a franchise right for YOU?

- Does the franchise have a unique strategic advantage (or disadvantage)?

- What location factors will determine how much money you take home?

- What are the most important issues you should research before you commit your funds?

- What is the real challenge in managing employees for the business?

- How dependent will your success be on implementing your own marketing and sales effort as opposed to the franchisor effort?

- What are the keys to creating a realistic business plan?

- How much should you invest in a franchise?

In this book, I'm going to reveal to you what many of us franchisees whisper about in the corner of the room when we gather together. Any of the 49 Insider Secrets you are about to learn could save you, or earn you, tens of thousands, or even hundreds of thousands of dollars.

My sole objective is to help you become financially successful if you decide to take this path. And to encourage you to take a different path if franchising is not a good match for you.

Along this journey, I have learned about the good, the bad, and the ugly of this business. You're going to hear how it is on the front lines. I watched as some highly qualified, motivated franchisees (myself included) struggled to make ends meet, and I observed others who have thrived. Which will it be for you? Only you can answer that question.

*-- **Mark Leonard***

Step 1 - Suitability

Your success in owning a franchise depends to a large degree on whether you are suited to the environment. It is fundamentally important that you clearly understand your personal strengths, desires, and challenges, and that you match your strengths and desires to the opportunity you are considering. Here are the areas of suitability that you should carefully consider before investing in a franchise:

- Your personality profile
- Your motivation
- Investment required
- Franchisor Profile
- Employee Profile
- Franchisee profile

Let's take a detailed look at each of these areas.

Your Personality

Just because a franchise has a wonderful reputation, and has produced many successful franchisees does NOT mean it is the right opportunity for you. You may be a highly creative person, and a rigidly structured environment might drive you crazy. Understanding your personality profile is the single most important step you must take before deciding to invest your hard-earned savings.

Action: Take a personality test

I suggest you (and your partner if you are going to have one) take a personality test, such as the Kolbe test, or the DISC test. These tests can reveal personality traits and action modes that you might not be otherwise able to articulate, which in turn can help you eliminate unsuitable opportunities, and focus on those franchises that closely match your personal strengths. Or the tests may reveal that franchises are not suited to you at all. I especially recommend the Kolbe test (www.kolbe.com).

Next, apply the results of your personality test very carefully to the franchise opportunities you are considering. Although franchises are offered in over 60 different categories, approximately 75% of the franchises owned today are restaurants.

> **Secret #1:** *To be a successful restaurant franchisee, you need to "follow the recipe". You cannot innovate, create new menu items, revise the décor, and most likely not even dictate the hours the franchise is open for business.*

Many franchisees appreciate this structure. If you are creative, though, it might drive you crazy. For me, it drove me crazy. We had a store in the middle of possibly the most sophisticated "foodie" city in the country, and we could NOT offer anything innovative to our customers. The local competition was running circles around us!

> **Action: On a scale of 1 – 10, score each opportunity you are considering as to how well it matches your personality profile.**

Your Motivation

You must clearly understand your motivation in buying a franchise. Are you tired of working for someone else, or angry because you are not advancing as fast as you think you deserve? Are you concerned that the field you are working in is at risk, and that you could be a victim? Would you be content working long hours in a business that you owned, and where the future is somewhat more secure? If so, you are essentially looking to buy a job. This is probably the most common reality of many franchises, and can be a very successful strategy.

> ***Secret #2:*** *Most franchisees are essentially "buying a job" with an average income range of $30,000 - $60,000 per year if 1) there is no debt; and 2) the franchisee works long hours in the business.*

On the other hand, you may be seeking to create significant wealth, in the multi-million dollar net worth category. To accomplish this in the franchise world, you will need to become a multi-unit owner or Area Developer. This will require a higher level of management skill, more capital, and investing in a franchise that encourages its successful franchisees to own multiple units. Often, this is a rapidly growing franchise, or an established franchise system with reasonably high density of locations.

Finally, you may be seeking to make money by buying under-performing locations, fixing them up, and flipping them.

> **Secret #3:** *If flipping businesses for profit is your goal, DO NOT BECOME A FRANCHISEE!*

My strong recommendation is to exercise this flipping strategy with privately held independent businesses, generally with sales starting in the $1-2MM annual sales range. The transaction costs are very high in smaller franchises, plus the franchisor creates a barrier to selling by requiring that the buyer become a franchisee prior to buying your business. If flipping is your passion, forget about franchises.

> **Action: Write down your primary motivation for buying a franchise. Then, on a scale of 1-10, match the franchise opportunity you are evaluating to your primary motivation.**

Your Money Situation

The third area of suitability is understanding how much cash is required to get to positive cash flow, taking into account both the amount you intend to personally invest, and the total amount to acquire the business, which may include financing (more on that later). Remember, you will likely make very little money during your first year to 18 months as you learn the business. Be sure to include your personal cost of living to the total investment required.

Now, here is some more controversial advice:

> ***Secret #4:*** *To maximize your likelihood of being successful, for your first franchise, pay ALL CASH ONLY!*

My strong advice is to avoid financing your first franchise. Loans are expensive (at this writing about 8-12% per annum and hard to get) and the term is short, requiring payments that can be crushing when you are first getting established. And by "avoid financing" I also mean DO NOT TOUCH YOUR 401K or any other retirement funds to buy your first franchise. These are risky investments (more on that later): if you have limited cash, buy a less expensive franchise. Any franchise directory will list franchises starting out at the low end with $10,000 -$25,000 required.

> **Action: Assign a score to the opportunities you are considering, where 1 = 75% or more financing required; 5 = seller financing at under 5% interest only for at least 5 years; and 10 = you have enough cash to pay for the entire investment.**

Other Franchisee Suitability

Take the vacation test. No, this doesn't mean flying off to the Caribbean and chilling out. In fact, forget about vacations for a couple of years. What this means is: get to know the other franchisees in the system. You're going to ask them lots of questions, and they will be your single most valuable resource before and during the time you own a franchise. Here's the Vacation Test.

> **Secret #5:** *Answer this question: "Would I (we) like to take a week-long vacation on a remote island with these franchisees?"*

If your answer is generally negative, consider another franchise, or another business.

The other factor to look at is how well the other franchisees are doing. Can they afford nice cars? Are they living in good neighborhoods? How much are they working in the business? Pay careful attention to how the other franchisees are doing economically.

Franchisor Suitability

What is the profile of the franchisor you are considering? Is it well-established with many successful franchise locations? Is the franchisor growing rapidly, leveling out, or shrinking in size? By the way, there is no right answer to that question.

> **Secret #6:** *A rapidly growing franchise might mean that the franchisor is sacrificing store profitability by putting locations too close together.*

Is the franchisor publicly held, part of a private-equity portfolio, or privately owned? What is the philosophy of the franchisor, especially with respect to franchisee relations? Is the franchisor constantly innovating, improving systems, and expanding the brand? Who is the CEO? How long has he/she been CEO, and what is their vision for the franchise? What are this person's strengths? As you answer these questions, compare the answers to your personality profile.

Action: On a scale of 1-10, how well does the franchisor profile match up with your personality profile?

Area Developer Suitability

Many established franchise systems have an Area Developer (AD) structure in place. The Area Developer is responsible for carrying out the franchisor's plan in their assigned territory. This includes recruiting franchisees, locating franchises in the territory, negotiating for locations, and insuring that franchisees are in compliance with franchisor rules and policies.

> ***Secret #7:*** *The Area Developer is your "Boss".*

I can hear you saying "But wait!!! I'm buying a franchise. I own my own business! I don't have a boss!"

OK, you don't have a boss, as long as you understand that the Area Developer can dictate your hours of business. He can and will dictate how many days per week you are open. He can walk in and inspect your business at any time, including your books and records, and can often levy penalties against you. Moreover, if in their judgment, you are not complying with the exact rules of the franchise, they can be responsible for taking your franchise away, and they can approve or deny who you can sell your franchise to. Sounds like a boss to me.

Therefore, it is extremely important that you ask these suitability questions about your new boss, I mean, Area Developer.

- Do you relate well to the Area Developer?

- What are the Area Developer's plans for the territory? More locations, more enforcement, more training, boosting store sales?

- What is the Area Developer's way of doing business? Supportive or aggressive? Training vs policing? Does the AD enjoy the support of most franchisees, or is the franchisee community highly politicized by the Area Developer?

- What is the process available to the franchisee if they feel that the Area Developer has not been fair to them?

- Can the Area Developer also be a franchisee? If yes, what are their plans for expansion, and how might that affect your plans? Who do you think will get the "cherry" locations if the Area Developer is also a franchisee?

- How is the Area Developer compensated? How much of the initial franchise fee do they get? What percentage of the royalty do they get if they sell you a new location, and how does that compare to the percentage they get if you buy an existing location?

Secret #8: *The Area Developer often gets a higher percentage of your revenue if they sell you a new location than if you buy an existing location. Therefore, they have a strong economic incentive to persuade you to build a new location.*

> ***Secret #9:*** *Owning a franchise is far more subject to political forces than owning an independent business.*

This last secret comes as a real shock to most new franchisees who believe the line about "owning their piece of the American Dream". The franchisee is not only subject to all the governmental laws, rules and policies governing the business, but is also subjected to the franchisor and Area Developer rules, agreements, policies, and procedures. The franchisor can arbitrarily choose to grant or deny requests by the franchisee to buy another franchise location, or to sell or re-locate their business, and many other critical areas. Just as in most Boss/Worker relationships, the Area Developer can make a franchisee's life pleasant, or difficult.

Employee Suitability

In this area of suitability, you need to get a clear understanding of the types of employees (if any) you will need to employ in your business. We examine this topic in more detail in Chapter 5, but here are some questions you need answers to about employees. What is their skill level? How much education do they need to have? How much turnover is normal in this business? How readily available is the type of labor you will require? What are the trends affecting the supply of the kinds of employees you will need?

Next, examine YOUR skills and background with respect to your understanding of the employees required. How well suited are you, by background or by training or by temperament, to manage the type of labor force you will require? For example, if you are a highly educated, white-collar professional, I would not recommend that you jump in on your first franchise to manage a large staff of blue-collar workers.

Step 2 - Trends

It is critical that you carefully research the trends affecting the opportunities you are considering at the following levels. I'm going to reveal some secrets for you in each of these areas.

- National trends
- Local trends
- Franchisor trends
- Employment trends
- Legal/governmental trends

National Trends

First, you must research the trends affecting your opportunity at a national level. Understand how the concept you are considering investing in may be affected by these trends. In 2014, some of the major trends we are seeing include the aging population, the massive changes in health care and health insurance laws, the weak but steady improvement in the economy, the threat of terrorism, the increasing economic power of immigrant groups in the US, especially Spanish-speaking populations, continued globalization, and rapid technology innovation and adoption.

> **Action: review past issues of the Wall Street Journal, The Economist, Business Week, Fortune Magazine, Entrepreneur, and other national business magazines for articles related to your opportunity.**

> **Action: Study the Bureau of Labor Statistics (http://www.bls.gov/) and Census data (http://www.census.gov/) for information that would relate to your opportunity.**

Local Trends

Once you have an idea about how the national trends may be affecting your opportunity, it is time to research how your geographic market may be different. In order to do this research, you need to dig up local information.

> **Action: Google "[your geographic location] economic outlook." Study reports that are relevant to the market for the opportunity you are considering.**

Now, uncover research that is even more specific to your particular opportunity. This is critical! For instance, I learned AFTER we bought into the Subway franchise that the San Francisco Bay Area has the lowest acceptance rate of Quick Service Restaurants (QSRs) in the country. This affects average store volume, and the population density that will support a profitable operation. With Subway corporate pushing for the same density in the Bay Area as in the rest of the country, this increases the probability of lower margin stores. There are many, many private research firms that provide consumer research in your area. For instance, Sandelman and Associates (http://www.sandelman.com/) provides excellent research in the foodservice arena. Another valuable resource is the Buxton company (http://buxtonco.com). This company performs a research analysis of the business potential of your exact location.

> **Secret #10:** *See if you can get local market research for free from the provider, or the franchisor, or from the franchisee association, or from an acquaintance at an ad agency serving customers in this area.*

Franchisor Trends

Now study how your Franchisor is doing. Answer the following questions at a minimum:

- How many locations does the franchisor have in its network?

- How many are franchisee-owned and how many are company-owned?

- How many new franchisee-owned stores have opened up in each of the last 5 years?

- How many new franchisor-owned stores have opened up in each of the last 5 years?

- How many franchisees have sold their stores, or shut down, in each of the last 5 years?

- What has been the AUV (average unit volume) for each of the last 5 years? Even better, knock off the results of the top 5-10% of stores. All franchises have super-star stores that do great volume. You're probably not going to get one of these. Therefore, by knocking off the cream, you can get a more realistic expectation of your results.

- What has been the trend in the average ticket for each of the last 5 years?

List the 5 closest competitors to your potential franchise. Compare your franchisor's growth rate to the growth rate of the competitors. Get the franchisor to articulate their growth plans both nationally and in your area.

Given the national and local trend knowledge you now have, is the franchisor's growth rate expectation realistic, in your opinion?

What significant developments have affected the franchisor in the last 3 years, such as executive personnel changes, major financing events, litigation, major change in operations, major changes in marketing? Have any major changes been announced but not yet implemented?

Is the franchise owned by a large corporation or private equity firm that has plans to "flip" the organization, and if so, can you project how that might affect your results?

Real Estate Trends

In some ways, the potential of your opportunity will be related to the trends in real estate in your area, both residential and commercial. Are people and businesses moving in or moving out? Are vacancy rates increasing or decreasing? Are commercial lease rates going up or down? You need to understand these trends, and how they will affect your business. If you are contemplating a home-improvement opportunity and your area is hit hard by lots of foreclosures, those factors may affect your projected sales volume.

> **Action: Contact local leading real estate brokerages, both residential and commercial, and ask for reports on the local real estate market.**

Get an idea of the local landlord perception of your franchise. If you are thinking about an opportunity that requires commercial real estate in which to operate, it is very important that you know how the landlord community regards your franchise. This will have an impact on how easy or difficult it will be to secure real estate, and how much you are likely to pay.

Secret #11: Take a knowledgeable Commercial Real Estate broker to lunch. Probe him or her on the general perception of the franchise, and ask the broker their opinion on the concept. What you learn may surprise you!

Employment Trends

You may have uncovered much of this information in your national and local research. Get more local information as it relates specifically to the types of employees you will require. Here are some more secrets to getting valuable information:

> ***Secret #12:*** *Wander around the neighborhood where you are most likely to acquire your business. How many "Help Wanted" signs do you see in the types of establishments that are employing your prospective employees?*

If you see many signs, you can be sure that 1) it will be quite difficult to recruit employees for your business; and 2) you will pay more for your employee compensation than you anticipated; and 3) your turnover is likely to be higher as other employers compete for your employees.

Legal/Governmental Trends

Before you invest in an opportunity, you need to have a clear understanding of the legal and governmental trends that may have an impact on your operations. Before you invest, answer the following questions:

How could recently enacted or proposed local, state, or national legislation affect your business? Pay special attention to:

Community development plans. The local politicians might be working with developers to improve a neighborhood. How could that affect the opportunity you are considering? Perhaps your neighborhood could suffer as another nearby neighborhood experiences significant renovation.

Employment legislation. For instance, San Francisco enacted legislation that required all employers to grant 1 hour of paid sick leave for every 30 hours worked, essentially increasing payroll costs by 3%. What are the trends that could affect your operation?

Regulation. How regulated will your business be? If you deal with hazardous materials, or food, or the elderly, or a lot of hourly workers, you need to factor in the costs of complying with regulations, and you need to anticipate which direction regulation is moving. For example, in the restaurant business, many communities are banning plastic bags and Styrofoam, and are moving towards banning any packaging which is not bio-degradable. Is your franchisor ahead of the curve on this, or are they burying their heads in the sand and hoping this trend goes away?

Permitting. Do you need special licenses or permits in order to operate? If so, how much do they cost, and how long does it take to get them, and are even more permit requirements on the way?

Step 3 - Location

The discussion of your franchise location may be the most controversial section of this book. The location of your business, especially if it requires commercial real estate, is THE MOST CRITICAL FACTOR IN YOUR SUCCESS. I say especially commercial real estate, but this discussion also applies even if you are going to be operating a home-based or vehicle-based business. We are going to take a careful look at:

- New locations

- Existing locations

- Leases and Landlords

- Assignments

New Locations

Here is possibly the most important, and most controversial, secret in this book:

> **Secret #13:** *If you are a first-time franchisee, DO NOT BUY OR BUILD A NEW LOCATION!*

This is exactly counter to what 99.9% of the franchisors and the "free" franchise brokers are trying to talk you into doing. This is an EXTREMELY DANGEROUS, EXTREMELY HIGH-RISK strategy. This is the secret that all of us know, even the ones who violated this principal and got lucky with a successful location.

Of course, the franchisor is going to tell you that their expertise and analysis will eliminate most of the risk in building a new location. They pay lots of money for demographic research that pinpoints exactly where a location will be successful. But remember, that computer program is going to give the answer the franchisor wants to hear, which may or may not be in the franchisee's best interest.

> **Secret #14:** *The strongest and most fundamental motivation of the franchisor is to get more system-wide sales. It is not to make franchisees profitable.*

Let's look carefully at the motivation, and risk, of the parties involved.

The franchisor makes money on your location from the day you open your doors. You may be losing money working 80 hours a week, but the franchisor will still be withdrawing their royalties and marketing funds from your bank account every week.

The franchisor has no financial risk in having you spend thousands or hundreds of thousands of your hard-earned dollars opening a new location. If it fails, you'll sell it at a steep loss to the next franchisee, and the franchisor keeps getting income.

> ***Secret #15:*** *If a franchisee is losing money, or sells their franchise and loses their investment, the franchisor does not report this is a failure! In fact, they will report the fact that the location has been successfully operating in that location for x years!*

The franchisor gets very little marginal, or new, income, if any, when a franchisee buys an existing franchise. But they get lots of marginal revenue when a new location opens. Therefore, what do they want you to do? Open up a new location, of course! In addition, the franchise brokers get nothing for recommending that you buy an existing business. Are they going to recommend that option to you? Not likely.

The franchisor will claim that the cost of building a new location is cheaper than buying an existing location. Maybe, maybe not. For those businesses that require commercial real estate, be sure to factor in the monstrous amount of time and money it will cost to find a location, negotiate the lease, get a reputable contractor, secure the proper permits and licenses, and hire and train a staff. Often, the franchisee gives up after chasing many locations that don't pan out. Many franchisors have had huge legal issues with accepting franchise fees from franchisees who couldn't find a location, and gave up, losing their franchise fee in the process.

> **Secret #16:** *Make sure you know exactly what the process is, if any, for recovering your franchise fee if the franchisor cannot or will not approve a location for you within a specified period of time.*

The fact is, if you are first-time franchisee, in spite of the franchisor's claims, you have no clue what it takes to be successful in your new business. You don't know what side of the street you need to be on, you don't know the dynamics of your customer base, or how to market to them, and you don't know how to recruit and train your employees.

If you are still tempted to build a new location after I have warned you, then at least please do the following:

> **Action: Test Drive your franchise. Go work in an existing franchise for at least 6 months, even as a laborer, even as an unpaid volunteer, before you buy or build a new location.**

Existing Locations

OK, so you are heeding my advice, and you are now considering only existing locations. There are still many, many dangers. You need to be well-armed with the following information before you buy.

Here is an important question to consider:

Would you relocate, out of your area, or even out of state, to buy a business? Oftentimes, this could make the difference between succeeding and failing.

> **Secret #17:** *Oftentimes the most profitable locations are the ones you would not suspect, such as small towns or tiny locations.*

Small, old, and a little run-down in a rural community often outperforms those high-volume locations in the middle of the city. Why? Lower rent, cost of labor, and the desirability of the product itself.

Once you start negotiating with a seller, it is important that you first understand what the sales picture is. What are the sales for the past 3 years? By sales, I mean documented sales.

- Get the sales reported on the seller's financial statements;

- Get the sales reported to the franchisor;

- Get the sales reported on the federal and state income tax returns;

- Get the sales reported on the sales tax returns.

Examine each of these reports carefully, and note any discrepancies. Grill the seller on any differences until you understand them completely.

If the seller is claiming that the sales are actually higher than the reports indicate because of some business process that the seller is employing (i.e., taking cash under the table), assign a value to this unreported amount as zero.

The seller's claims of unreported sales are worthless to you. There is no way to verify this amount; the seller is subject to prosecution by the IRS and by the franchisor; and you may or may not choose to employ the same practice under your ownership. The seller got his or her benefit in tax-free and royalty-free cash: they do not also get the benefit of applying those unreported dollars to the selling price.

- What is the sales trend? Is it up, down, or sideways? What is the stack-ranking of your location compared to others in your market? What does your trend research tell you about the likelihood of sales increasing or decreasing?

- What is the cost of goods sold? What are the trends? The dramatic increase in fuel prices over the last several years has affected the underlying cost of nearly everything in the supply chain these days, from food to plastics to transportation. Has pricing been able to keep up with rising costs of goods? Again, match the reported cost of goods sold from the seller's financial statements to the tax returns, and understand any discrepancies.

- What is the cost of labor? Analyze your projected labor costs very carefully.

Secret #18: *Be sure to find out if the Seller is employing family, and paying under the table, therefore under-reporting the true cost of labor. Is the spouse doing all the books, are the children working, etc.?*

How is your trend research from Section #2 going to impact your labor costs? Do not apply a simple "rule-of-thumb" percentage. Create or examine an actual labor schedule, and factor in the increasing cost of your labor, adjusted especially by anticipated future regulatory costs. Be sure to account fully for the hours you will work in the business, and the amount the seller is working in the business.

> **Secret #19:** *If you plan to work LESS in the business than the current owner does, you obviously need to increase the labor cost. AND, you need to adjust projected sales down, and increase your cost of goods.*

There is no-one who will care about customer service and sales, and cost of goods, as much as the owner.

If you plan on working MORE than the current owner, do NOT agree to revalue the net income stream for the improvements to sales and cost of goods you may achieve. If the current owner is an absentee owner, and you plan on working 50 hours a week in the business, it is OK to assume that your labor cost will go down, but not by the full 50 hours. Assume you may be able to eliminate labor on 50-75% of your time on the schedule.

What is the cost of utilities? Here are some of the utilities you need to consider:

- Electricity
- Gas
- Water
- Garbage
- Phone

- Internet bandwidth

- Music service

- Video or cable service

- WiFi service

- Alarm system

- Camera (surveillance) system

Understand thoroughly how utility costs are assigned to you. Will you pay each of them from separate meters? Or are some utilities paid for by the landlord and then shared and allocated pro-rata among several tenants? Or does the landlord pay some or all of the utilities? What is the trend in the cost of utilities? Will you have to make upgrades to any of the utilities in the future?

For example, Subway recently required all franchisees to acquire high speed toaster ovens which required 220 volt service. Some locations didn't have enough electrical capacity to add this service to their stores, and they were forced to spend big bucks to bring this service in.

Are you going to have to invest in technology to support your operations? Will you be required to provide WiFi hotspots, or flat-screen TVs, High Speed internet T1 lines, or DSL for processing? If that capability is not currently in your store, factor in the cost of providing it. What about surveillance? If the location you are considering does not have it yet, get it, and get the high-speed internet connection too so you can view what's going on in your location even when you're not there. Technology is available that enables you to view the output from surveillance cameras directly and clearly on your cell phone.

What is the cost of equipment repairs? If you are following my advice and buying an existing location, you need to be very, very careful in evaluating any existing equipment. Is any of it under warranty? How much is the owner currently spending on repairs?

> **Action: List every piece of equipment in the location that would cost over $500 to replace, and assign a best guess as to when you will need to replace that equipment. Build these costs into your Business Plan.**

Remember, you may have to replace equipment not just because it is not working, but the franchisor may demand you replace equipment for any or no good reason. Or you may want to replace a piece of equipment that is working okay because it is hogging too much electricity. Add a yearly amount to the equipment repair cost that would cover the cost of replacing old or obsolete equipment.

When are you going to have to remodel the location? Most franchisors require that the franchisees update the look of their location periodically. It is critical to understand where in this cycle the location is, and when you will be required to remodel your location, and approximate what the costs of the remodel will be.

> **Secret #20:** Be sure to ask the franchisor what their plans are for requiring an upgrade to the POS system or other technology initiatives, and what their cost estimate is. This can often be a $20,000 investment.

What are your lease costs? A special place in the franchisee torture-chamber is reserved for you if you are not completely aware of the details and intricacies of the lease you would assume in acquiring an existing business. That subject is next.

Leases and Landlords

If the business you are acquiring requires commercial space, and you must lease it (as opposed to purchasing it), the success of your business often rides on the terms of the commercial lease. If you just close your eyes and hope that everything will turn out nice and then sign the lease or lease assumption without thoroughly understanding every single clause, you may likely fail in the future. The realm of the commercial lease is unregulated and tilted strongly toward the landlord's advantage. Buyer beware.

The reality is that most small commercial tenants negotiate a commercial lease only once every 5 to 10 years. On the other hand, landlords negotiate leases every day. Their business, their income, and the value of their property depends upon squeezing the most money they can out of every single lease, so they are experts at it. They employ top notch real estate brokers, property managers, and real estate attorneys to make sure the lease terms are as one-sided as possible. Most landlords will accumulate as much power as possible through the lease: they take the "-lord" part of their title very seriously.

Many books have been written about the commercial lease: it is wise to read one or two if you are entering into a substantial obligation. Remember, once you enter into a long-term lease, there is almost never any clean way of getting out early. Did you find out that you are paying significantly more than your neighboring tenants? Is your business not as profitable as you projected, and now you're working long hours just to make that lease payment? Would a minor and temporary rent reduction help you get back on your feet? Thinking about closing down or relocating because you just can't make it at your present location? Tough – your landlord will likely bring the full force of the legal system down on you if you miss one payment. The ability of your business to produce income depends to a large degree on the lease terms.

> **Secret #21:** *The value of the business, if you ever intend to sell it, depends to a large degree on the lease terms.*

The income you make and the lease terms are completely different aspects: you could have a favorable, low rent payment that enables you to make good money, but the lease is personal to you, and if you attempted to sell the business, the landlord could require completely different terms which could substantially destroy the value of the business. In that situation, you are trapped.

There are several major concepts that you need to know in order to have the lease work in your favor, and not against you.

First, you need to have complete neutrality with respect to both the business opportunity and the location. If you love the business and the location, but the landlord will not grant you terms that you can feel comfortable with, WALK AWAY. Go buy another franchise location.

Second, view any lease negotiations that you engage in as a process – not an event. Take your time, be patient, expect to get your proposals rejected at first.

Third, don't just focus on the rent payment: there are about 30 other terms you need to negotiate, many of which can have a significant economic impact on the overall lease costs. For instance, it may be very important to the landlord to receive a very high rent per square foot, in fact, way over market. That may be OK: he may be willing to trade this off by offering substantial free rent and/or tenant improvement (TI) allowances. I know about a tenant who negotiated 4 years of free rent on a 10 year lease!

Here are some of the key terms you need to thoroughly understand before you sign a lease or lease assumption:

- **Name of tenant** Is it you personally, or your business entity? Is it the Franchisor, with you, the franchisee, being a sub-lessee?

- **Permitted Use** Be careful that the permitted use is specific. I know about a Subway store whose landlord forced the franchisee to spend $80,000 on a specialized scrubber/venting system because another tenant didn't like the smell of freshly baked bread in the morning. This problem could have been solved if the lease stated that the tenant was going to be baking fresh bread every day, and that this would create the smells of fresh bread.

- **Exclusive Use** If you are in a shopping center or other multi-tenant location, is the landlord permitted to rent to a competitor of yours? Is that OK with you?

- **Number of square feet** How much do you have? Understand the difference between usable and rentable square feet.

- **The term of the lease** How many months from the Commencement Date does the lease run?

- **Early termination** Under what circumstances could either the tenant or the landlord terminate the lease?

- **Fixturing period** How much time is the landlord giving you to build out or remodel? Is this period free of all rent, or will you have to pay CAM charges and utilities?

- **Commencement date** What is the date that the lease officially begins? Is it at all tied to being open for business, or is it when you sign the lease, or somewhere in between?

- **Tenant Improvement Allowance** How much is the landlord giving you in tenant improvement allowances? When is it paid, and do you get reimbursed, or does the Landlord directly pay the contractors?

Secret #22: Landlords will frequently grant a tenant improvement allowance upon lease renewal.

- **Security Deposit** How much is it? Can you amortize this down over time, and conditional on good performance?

- **Personal Guarantee** Is a guarantee required? Is it personal, or given by the business? How much is it for? Can this be reduced or negotiated away over time?

- **Base Minimum Rent** It is important that you understand how this is calculated. Many landlords today are trying to get away from having the rent based on number of square feet. Be very careful.

- **Percentage Rent** Many landlords, especially in shopping centers, will attempt to get extra rent based on your sales volume. This will involve monthly reporting of your sales results, sending in copies of your sales tax returns, and is nearly always accompanied by the landlord dictating the minimum days and hours you must be open.

- **CAM (Additional Rent) charges** CAM stands for Common Area Maintenance. Be sure you understand the components (property tax, insurance, utilities, janitorial, management, etc.) and what your pro-rata share is.

- **Rent Escalation** This is always negotiable, and ranges from no increases during the term of the lease, to periodic fixed percentage increases, to increases based on one of the CPI indexes.

- **Options to extend the lease** If you intend to occupy your location for an extended period, or if you plan to sell the business at some point, you may want options to extend the lease. Sometimes, the landlord may be willing fix the pricing for those options if you fight for it, and sometimes the landlord will insist on "market rate" at the time you renew. Either way can work to the tenant's advantage. Sometimes the uncertainty created by a "market rate" clause enables a more in-depth negotiation at lease renewal time

- **Business Hours** A landlord often times couples prescribed business hours with percentage rent in order to make sure the location is grossing as much as possible. Be extremely cautious: there can often be serious financial penalties for not being open during the prescribed hours, even if those hours are unprofitable to the store.

- **Parking** Do you have assigned or designated parking for your location? Be sure to assess the availability of parking for both your customers and employees.

- **Signage** Many tenants are shocked to learn that the landlord may insist on extra charges to locate signage, especially on a pylon or monument sign. Be sure to cover this in your negotiations.

- **Relocation/Expansion rights** For locations in a shopping center of any size, the landlord often reserves the right to move the tenant's location at will to somewhere else in the shopping center, sometimes even making the tenant bear some or all of the cost of the move. This can be devastating to the business.

- **Assignment Rights** This is a very dangerous area that needs its own separate discussion, as follows.

Assignments: Landlord

Lease assignment clauses are the tools that landlords use to exercise an enormous amount of control over the value of the business, and by extension, over the franchisee. Almost all leases require the permission of the Landlord to assign the rights and responsibilities of the lease to someone else. If the Landlord wants to unreasonably deny an assignment, you are likely to lose the buyer before you can successfully prosecute the matter in court.

Many leases specify that the lease is personal to the lessee, meaning that when you sell the business, all terms of the lease, including the rent, term, security deposit, and CAM charges, are up for re-negotiation with the Landlord. Therefore, the under-market rent you are now enjoying which enables you to make a nice profit could disappear if you wanted to sell the business to someone else, therefore wiping out the value of the business. In addition, the Landlord frequently reserves the right to charge you significant fees to go through the assignment process.

> ***Secret #23:*** *Most assignments do not allow the original tenant (you) to be released from the obligation to pay the rent even with an assignment.*

What this means is that if your buyer stops paying rent for any reason, the Landlord will come after you. Not only that, if the reason that the rent isn't being paid is because your buyer is mis-managing the business, you may not have the ability to go in and take over the business because you may no longer be a qualified franchisee after you have sold the business. Can you see how this could put you in a mess?

You must understand and acknowledge these very real risks. I had a client almost lose an $800,000 sale of his franchise because one of the landlords refused to assign the lease to the buyer even though she was a fully qualified franchisee of the system, with a career and education in the same line of work as the franchise. Plus, she qualified for a big SBA loan and she was putting a lot of cash into the purchase price. Even though the Landlord ultimately relented under the threat of legal action, the seller is forced to live with his existing guarantee on the lease for the next 4 years. If that buyer fails, he will have to make lease payments that could wipe him out economically because he wouldn't be able to take over the business.

> **Action: Make sure any lease assignment clause requires the landlord to automatically grant a full assignment to any fully qualified franchisee of the system.**

Full assignment means release of all liabilities related to the performance of the lease. Better yet, have the franchisor sign the lease with the right to place whatever tenant they want to in the location.

Assignments: Franchisor

Lease assignment clauses apply only to those concepts that require commercial space, but all franchise concepts have assignment clauses restricting your ability to sell your franchise. This acts as a very significant drag on your ability to sell your business if you want to or need to, as the buying process follows these minimum steps.

First, you must find someone who wants the business in your location. They have to be sold not only on the location, but the franchise system too.

Then, they must become authorized franchisees of the system, typically by filling out an application, taking a test, receiving the FDD (Franchise Disclosure Document, formerly known as UFOC and other disclosure documents, signing the Franchise Agreement, paying a franchise fee and attending training. This can be a time-consuming and a high hurdle.

Story: I had a buyer for one of my stores who was a very successful convenience store and gas station owner with over $1,000,000 in cash, and he offered me a fair price, all cash, for my franchise. Even though he was clearly a successful businessman, he failed the Math Test that Subway required, and was denied a franchise.

The next step is that the Franchisor must approve the new franchisee to buy YOUR franchise. Believe it or not, the Franchisor may attempt to talk your buyer into another location, or may deny the assignment because the new franchisee isn't experienced enough to buy your franchise location, or because they live too far away, or other reasons.

Then, the Franchisor will likely require significant documentation and procedures to be followed in order to close escrow, and their transfer department may take weeks to authorize a sale. During this time, your buyer could get cold feet and back out of the deal, or events could happen in your franchise to reduce the value to the buyer.

Finally, the Franchisor will assess an assignment fee, oftentimes significant, to enable you to sell your business. And then, as we discussed above, if the buyer, after they buy your franchise, should default on any of their obligations that affect you, including lease payments or seller financing, you probably won't have the ability to repossess the business because you are no longer an authorized franchisee.

> ***Secret #24:*** *Thoroughly understand the Franchisor's assignment process BEFORE you agree to buy a franchise, and accept that selling a franchise involves significantly more "friction", ancillary costs, and time, than selling an independent business.*

Step 4 - Due Diligence

It is imperative that you conduct a thorough due diligence process to uncover as many of the risks that you can before you buy your franchise. Failing to uncover some of these risks can jeopardize the success of your purchase. This due diligence includes reading and re-reading the entire FDD, focusing especially on certain aspects discussed below.

There are a number of excellent resources that detail how you should conduct due diligence, especially on franchise opportunities. I strongly recommend that you invest in one of these systems for a comprehensive guide to conducting this critical area of research. One of the best systems I have seen is located at http://diomo.com. In the meantime, here are my recommendations.

Litigation

It sounds boring and dry, but read Item 3 of the FDD (Litigation History) very carefully. Understand that bringing legal action against a franchisor is extremely expensive and time-consuming, and would only be the end-result of a long history of a failure to communicate and co-operate. Read each case: what can you learn? Could the subjects of the lawsuits affect you? Is there a lot of litigation or a little?

> **Secret #25:** *If there is a lot of litigation listed in the FDD that has occurred or is still pending within the last 2 years, avoid this opportunity.*

It doesn't matter how successful the franchise appears to be, or how many awards they've gotten from Entrepreneur magazine, or even if the franchisor has won all the lawsuits. The franchise is not being managed in a co-operative way.

Franchisee Obligations

Read this section (Item 9) very carefully too. Notice how long the list is, especially when compared to the Franchisor obligations. Count on the Franchisor enforcing in detail every obligation listed in this section. For instance, many franchisors require you to be open a minimum number of hours per week, even if you are demonstrably losing money during some of those hours. That may be one of the costs of owning that particular franchise.

> **Secret #26:** *Note the obligations that surprise you. When you speak with existing and former franchisees, be sure to discuss these specific obligations, and how diligently they are enforced by the franchisor.*

If you are getting the impression from reading Item 9 that owning this franchise is more restrictive and subject to more rules than your current job, pay attention to that. Then ask yourself, referring back to your Personality Profile, whether you will thrive, in the long run, living with these Franchisee Obligations.

Territory

Read Item 12 very carefully. Is the franchisor offering you a protected territory? If so, at what cost - in other words, how much, if any, in sales are you required to produce?

Also, you may have a protected territory, but does the franchisor reserve the right to locate competing, but differently branded, franchises within your territory? If you have no protected territory, is the franchisor protecting your investment in any way? For instance, do they have a review process before establishing a competing franchise near you? Do you have the right of first refusal to develop a location near you?

Go back to your Trend Research: is the franchisor actively developing, and if so, what has been the impact of their development on store operations and profitability?

Consider this example: if a store has a breakeven of $9,000 in sales per week, and is currently doing $12,000, it might be quite profitable. Then, the franchisor authorizes another location within blocks of the existing location, and now both locations produce $9,000 per week in sales. This is a big win for the franchisor, which has just increased their sales by nearly 50%, but now two franchisees are struggling to make breakeven. Be very careful: this happens all the time.

> **Secret #27:** Even if you don't have territory protection from the franchisor, examine whether you have protection from outside forces.

This might be governmental restrictions from surrounding communities or districts that prohibit additional locations of your type of business, non-compete clauses in a shopping mall, or population restrictions that render it very unlikely that another franchisee would be foolish enough to invest in a nearby location.

Franchisee Research

In Item 20, the franchisor must identify the name, address and phone number of at least 100 current franchisees; and the number of franchises it anticipates selling in the next year. Determine the number of franchises in the last 3 fiscal years that have been transferred, cancelled, terminated, not renewed or reacquired by the franchisor. Get the name, home address and phone number of every franchisee who voluntarily or involuntarily ceased to be a franchisee during the last year, or who has not communicated with the franchisor within 10 weeks of the application date. This will also provide information about the number of company units.

There is gold in talking with the listed franchisees.

> **Secret #28:** Schedule your talks with the ex-franchisees: call every single one, up to 50 of them.

Ask them why they left the system, how much they invested, whether they made a profit in the system, and the reasons they either succeeded or failed. Find out how their relations were with the franchisor, any area developers, and with their franchisee peers.

> **Secret #29:** *Find out hidden information from ex-franchisees. Ask the ex-franchisees who the formal and informal leaders are, and ask to borrow past years' copies of FDD's.*

Review the cancellations, transfers, and terminations numbers. What are they as a percent of the overall number of locations? If you have prior year's FDDs or UFOCs, compare these percentages to prior years. Is it going up or down?

Next, call and visit as many existing franchisees as possible. Before you call, understand what the peak hours of the business are, and call either about an hour before or after the peak hours, and ask to speak with the owner. Don't bother leaving a message if the owner isn't available: most of the time the message won't get delivered. When you get the owner on the line, introduce yourself, and let the owner know you are a prospective franchisee and that you are doing your due diligence, and ask them for either a face-to-face meeting for about 20-30 minutes at a time that is convenient to them or a telephone interview. You might be surprised at not only how many owners will be glad to meet with you: many may also offer you their franchise, or at least know owners who are selling their franchise!

Secret #30: *Many existing franchisees will shade their answers to your questions to the positive side. Why? Because they may want to sell to you, or they are afraid of retribution by the franchisor or Area Developer if word got back that they were expressing negative sentiments about the business. READ BETWEEN THE LINES!*

Here are some of the questions you must ask the existing franchisees:

- How long have they owned the franchise location?

- Do they own just one or more units?

- Have the financial results for each location met their expectations?

- Ask what percentage each major expense category currently is, e.g. for a restaurant – food cost, labor cost, rent, and utilities.

- Ask them what the average sales volume is per franchise location.

- Ask them if they have an idea about the characteristics of a location that exceeds the average, and why some locations are below average.

- Find out how much the average ticket is, and whether this is trending up or down. What are the factors influencing the average ticket?

- Ask whether they believe the future is trending up or down for the market in general for the franchise products.

- Find out who the main competition is, and whether competition is getting weaker or stronger. Ask about both franchise and non-franchise competitors.

- How much labor is required, and what are the pay rates, and how easy or hard is it to find, recruit, train, and retain the requisite employee pool?

- Ask how much interaction they have with other franchisees, and whether they get value from associating with other franchisees.

- Ask them whether they know of any organizational trends or changes taking place at the franchisor.

- Ask about the quality of the training provided by the franchisor.

- Ask about the relationship they have with the Area Developer. This is extremely important! It is surprising how political owning a franchise can be. Some franchisors and Area Developers are fairly hands-off, and some are extremely detail oriented.

- Ask them whether they think the franchisor is headed in the right direction, and the improvements they would like the franchisor to make.

- Very important: ask them how the formal relations are between the franchisee community and the franchisor. Ask them if they are aware of any litigation, especially pending litigation.

- Ask what the purchasing methodology is for both Cost of Goods Sold, and for other materials used in the business, especially marketing and sales materials.

- Ask them how many hours per week they currently work in and on the business.

- Ask them what the biggest mistake and/or surprise they have experienced.

- Ask them what is the biggest challenge they currently face.

- Ask them if they would buy the franchise again.

- Ask them what important question have you missed.

Be sure to keep extensive notes of each interview you conduct, and be sure to ask each franchisee for permission to stay in touch with them.

After you have conducted 6-10 interviews, step back and ask yourself whether you really enjoyed the company of the franchisee-owners. Do they share much in common with you in terms of values and attitudes? Think about our first lesson: are they people you would like to associate with?

Franchisee Relations

Now you have some good information from the FDD, from ex-franchisees, and from current franchisees about the relationship between franchisor and franchisees.

Your next step: Call the head of the Franchisee Association, and ask directly for his/her assessment of the relationship, and the pressures on the relationship.

Typically, this is a volunteer organization, and the person who has organized and leads this organization is passionate and energetic about the business. Spend as much time as you can with this individual to assess the dynamics of the business. Again, read between the lines.

Franchisor Training and Inspections

From your interviews, you will now have a pretty good idea of the training and the inspections the franchisor conducts. Talk with the Area Developer and the VP Operations about trends in these two areas. Specifically, ask the following questions:

- What is the franchisor doing to move training to an online, web-based model?

- How frequently is the franchisee required to attend offsite training, especially that which requires plane flights and hotel rooms?

- What is the franchisor doing to increase the scope of training?

- What is the franchisor doing to for providing training for ESL employees?

- What are the trends in their inspection process? Are they enforcement oriented, or training oriented? Is there congruence between what the franchisor is reporting and what the franchisee community is reporting?

Purchasing Methodology

It is extremely critical that you understand how you are going to be acquiring the materials you use in your business. This refers to:

- Cost of Goods Sold; and

- Marketing, Sales, and Administrative materials.

This varies all over the map. Some franchisors require that you purchase all raw materials from them, some license or authorize certain vendors, and some specify the materials you must buy but you are on your own to find suppliers.

Caution. It is very dangerous when a franchisor is also selling product to the franchisee community: this typically means that not only is the franchisee paying a royalty to the franchisor, but that the franchisor is also making a monopolistic profit on the purchases by the franchisees, driving up costs and reducing profits. Several years ago, Quiznos was operating under this model, and were basically forced to change their model after many franchisee lawsuits.

Also, find out about the restrictions and processes for conducting marketing and sales campaigns. Does the franchisor provide these materials, or do they specify what you may and may not use? Does the franchisor require approval for every sales and marketing campaign, and if so, how responsive is the franchisor in responding to franchisee requests. Does the franchisor tolerate or encourage local-market adjustments, or are they inflexible? It is imperative that you know these characteristics in advance of signing a Franchise Agreement.

Competition

This is a very big consideration that you MUST know inside out before committing your funds to a franchise.

1. Understand the franchise competitors; and
2. Understand the competitors who are NOT franchises.

Here is the Big Secret Deal about the second point above.

> ***Secret #31:*** *Don't buy a franchise, any franchise, unless you can make a lot more money than non-franchise competitors.*

Remember, you will pay a premium for the franchise, you will be very limited in your ability to adjust to local market conditions, and you will have serious restrictions if you decide to sell your business. The only way this can possibly make sense is if you are making a TON of money that your competitors cannot touch.

Here's a real-life story. Our first Subway location was located in the heart of San Francisco's Financial District. We had 30,000 office workers within 500 feet of our location. We had customers lining up out the door every lunch.

And we were getting killed by our competitors.

Here's what I learned. Our competitors were typically higher-end delis that were open from around 8am and closed at 3pm, and worked only from Monday through Friday. We were REQUIRED to be open 7 days a week, for 98 hours, and we could only close 3 days per year. They were working 35 hours, and never on weekends and holidays. And guess what else? Our food costs on a per unit basis were lower, but their average ticket was double ours! So, our competitors had much lower labor costs, lower food costs, had no royalty overhead, and had daily sales that were way in excess of ours. We learned too late that we had bought into a system that virtually GUARANTEED our competitors would make more money than our franchise.

Don't let this happen to you!

Here's what you need to do.

> **Action: Go talk to 5-10 of your potential franchise competitors, asking them the same questions as you asked franchisees of the system you are considering (above).**
>
> **Action: Go talk to 5-10 of your non-franchise competitors, asking them the same questions.**

When you have accomplished this amount of Due Diligence, you are now one SMART and SAVVY entrepreneur.

Step 5 - Employees

Skill Sets Required

Many, if not most, franchises available today, require that you recruit, hire, train, and retain employees. In order to be successful, you need to thoroughly understand the entire employee process, and how it impacts your business and your success.

> ***Secret #32:*** *Just because your concept requires low-paid employees, you cannot assume that it will be easy to find such employees.*

Let's discuss this through an example. Many of the franchise concepts that require low-paid employees are in the food industry and related retail concepts. It is a common misconception that employees for these establishments can be "unskilled" labor and that there is a plentiful supply. In fact, the opposite is true. Most retail concepts require that their employees can do all, or at least most, of the jobs required in the establishment. This means not only cleaning and washing dishes, but also food preparation, cashiering, and serving customers. Each of these areas requires thorough attention to detail, reliability, teamwork, diligent work effort, a ready smile, good language skills, a willingness to learn new skills, and good physical condition. If ANY of these characteristics are missing, your business – and you – will suffer.

Now, take a moment to think about each of these characteristics. How easy will it be to find someone to work at or near minimum-wage, who exhibits:

- Reliability
- Speed and productivity
- Willing and able to learn
- Teamwork
- Excellent customer service
- Good physical condition
- Excellent language skills

Let me ask you a question: if an individual exhibited all of these characteristics, are they really forced to work at minimum wage? If not, how much are you realistically going to pay employees to get these characteristics?

> **Action: Using your interviews with franchisees, ex-franchisees, Area Developers, and the franchisor, make a list of ALL the skills required of your employees. If there are several positions, create this list for each position.**

Next, for each position, create a list of sources where you are likely to find employees for this position, e.g. Craigslist, community college job boards, websites, signs in your window, churches, other employees, etc. Look at each of these sites, and determine what kind of demand there is: who is your competition for these employees, and how much are they paying?

> **Secret #33:** *Right now, many QSR's are hurting for employees because of the enormous competition from the coffee stores, like Starbucks.*

How can a QSR retain good employees at near minimum wage when Starbucks is starting employees out at $12-14 per hour, plus tip income, plus health-care benefits, plus enormous schedule flexibility?

Do this same exercise if your franchise concept requires a higher level of skills, and education. Again, be realistic about how readily available you can find employees that match your requirements.

> **Secret #34:** *During those inevitable times when you lose key employees, YOU will be filling in, GUARANTEED.*

Oh, and those times will occur at the time that is most inconvenient to you: when your child's recital is taking place, when you were planning to go to (or host) that ripping party, or when you were just planning to get away for a day. Or when you were about to leave on that needed retreat at the beach.

On-site or Absentee

Almost all franchisors pitch their "business-in-a-box" concept: they have written all the procedures, so that all you have to do is follow the formula, and - VOILA! – the American dream is yours. Unfortunately, this cultivates a sense that the franchise can be run with an absentee owner. Read between the lines: you will hear that the business is simple to run. This does NOT mean that it is EASY! Big distinction!

> ***Secret #35:*** *I don't know of ANY franchises that can be run successfully with absentee owners.*

Even the highly successful multi-unit owners that I know who are pulling down big incomes work the business extremely hard, 40-60 hours per week or more.

> ***Secret #36:*** *If you are buying your first franchise, you MUST plan on working the business full-time (50-70 hours per week) for the first year.*

I don't care if you are buying a franchise that has been running on remote control with a superb manager for 2 years. If you don't get in there and work the business so that you understand every detail, you WILL LOSE MONEY! Either your key employees will quit, or they will hold you up for more money, or your customers will change and you won't understand why your sales are declining.

Family

Having multiple members of your family working in the franchise is a big discussion. Have a crystal clear plan and understanding about how the business is going to involve your family, and be as objective and realistic as you can about the rewards - and the risks – of family involvement.

Action: Take the skills list from the exercise above, and match up your family members to those positions.

Do they fit? If not, do yourself a favor, and do NOT demand, require, expect, or coerce your family members into working the business. It may be your dream, and it may NOT be theirs. Lifelong conflict could arise if you try to force this issue.

Action: If you think your family members would be a good match for the business, then have a serious discussion with each member about the role you see them playing, and whether they are motivated to play that role.

Ask these questions:

If a spouse: Is he or she going to quit their existing job to take on this role? Would he or she like this work more or less than his or her current job? Would he or she make more or less money in the franchise as in their current job? Can the two of you tolerate working closely together? Do you have complementary skills, or will you both gravitate to the same tasks? Is your overall financial risk increased or reduced if your spouse gives up their current employment?

If a child: Is your child motivated to work in the business? What would they be giving up to work in the business: participation in a school sport or other activity, extra classes, the development of other skills, etc.? How well will they relate to you as "Boss", which is a lot different from "Parent?" How successful have you been at resolving conflict amicably in the past? What will be the risk to your relationship if you must fire your child? Would you have the strength to do this?

Story: The most gut-wrenching, difficult experience I had as a franchisee was when I discovered that my then 19-year-old son swiped $5.00 from the cash register, and then denied it. Of course, I would have given it to him if he had asked, and I would have forgiven him if he had owned up to it, but he didn't. So I fired him. It hurt us both extremely deeply, and I didn't hear from him for 6 months. Fortunately, we have since re-established a close relationship.

Are you prepared for this experience? If the honest answer is "No", then do not hire a family member.

If a parent or other relation: Again, does that person have the skills required for the role? Many jobs require speed and good physical shape to do well. Does your other relation have what it takes? Also, how will they relate to you in the role of "Boss"? Are they going to take direction from you easily? What are they giving up to work for you? What if things don't go as well as planned: how will that affect your role in the overall family? Is it worth the risk?

Family Upside

Despite the caution encouraged above, there is upside to working with family. For one thing, if you work well together, it could bring you closer together. Also, talk with your accountant, but there are definitely ways to structure the business that can reduce the burden of employer taxes, thus lowering your overall labor costs, and increasing your probability of success.

Workers Comp

Workers' Compensation insurance, for many businesses, is a huge expense. It is imperative that you study this aspect of your business thoroughly. Here are the questions you must have clear answers to:

- What are the market forces affecting Workers Comp rates for the employees you will have?

- Is your state legislation attracting more carriers, or driving them out?

- Are rates going up, or are they going down?

Be sure to build these trends into your business plan.

If you are looking at an existing franchise (my recommendation), are the current Workers Comp rates correct? I've seen them incorrectly classified, resulting in both higher and lower rates than necessary. Be sure to shop around, especially at annual renewal times. Sometimes your carrier may want to get out of the market, and will raise rates dramatically as one part of the strategy to exit the market.

Be sure to discuss these issues with a qualified Workers Comp insurance person.

Health Care

We all know that Health Care insurance is one of the most prominent issues in the country. Costs are increasing, and the ACA legislation and changing requirements are going to make the market fairly chaotic for a long time.

You must understand both your short-term and long-term position with respect to providing your employees with health care benefits, and you must understand the legislative environment that may affect you.

Ask (and answer) these questions:

- What percentage of other franchisees in the system offers their employees health-care benefits? Which employees get health-care: all employees, or just certain positions?

- How rapidly are health-care costs escalating?

- Does the franchisor offer access to low-cost health-care insurers, or is everything being migrated to the ACA exchanges?

- What percentage of your competitors, both franchise and non-franchise, offer health-care benefits?

- What is the local government (city, county) doing about health-care? In San Francisco, they have passed a law requiring all employers of 20 or more employees to either provide health-care benefits, or pay the city government an extra $1.55 or more per hour worked! That could add 15% to labor costs: will all franchises be able to pass those extra costs along to the consumer?

- What is the state government doing about health-care? What impact will this have on your business?

Sick-leave, PTO

Be sure to have a clear understanding of whether you will offer your employees paid sick leave or paid/unpaid Personal Time Off (PTO). Just because the franchise you are considering for acquisition is not offering these benefits doesn't mean you can't or won't.

These questions are similar to the health-care questions. Again, be sure to build your knowledge and answers into your business plan.

- What percentage of other franchisees in the system offer their employees sick leave and PTO benefits? Which employees get sick-leave and PTO: all employees, or just certain positions?

- What percentage of your competitors, franchise and non-franchise, offer sick leave and PTO benefits?

- What is the local government (city, county) doing about sick leave and PTO? In San Francisco, they have passed a law requiring all employers to provide paid sick-leave benefits at a rate of 1 hour for each 30 hours worked! That adds about 3% to the payroll costs: will all franchises be able to pass those extra costs along to the consumer?

- What is the state government doing about sick leave and PTO? What impact will this have on your business?

Other Benefits

Think about other benefits that you will consider providing your employees, such as:

- Paid vacation
- Education benefits
- Matching contributions to certain charities
- Company automobile
- Holiday parties
- End-of-year bonuses
- Company trips
- Additional training, both on-site and off-site

What impacts will the cost of these possible other benefits have on your business? Will you be able to develop a competitive advantage by offering these benefits? Will that benefit offset the cost of the benefit?

Be sure to think through these other benefits carefully before you decide to buy that franchise.

Wage Trends

You must have a clear understanding of wage trends for the employees you will need for your business. Research the following:

What is the unemployment rate in your county? How does it compare with surrounding counties, and with the state? If your overall unemployment rate is lower, you will have a relatively more difficult time attracting employees, and your costs will be higher to retain good employees.

> ***Secret #37:*** *It is almost impossible to hire reliable, hard-working workers in affluent communities, even at high wages.*

The children of the wealthy homeowners won't want to and don't need to work at low paying jobs, and surrounding labor pools may not have the means or desire to commute into the wealthier community.

What are the educational trends in your locale? Is enrollment at the community colleges going up or down?

How do mandated increases in the minimum wage affect your costs? Can your business keep up with the rate of increase anticipated?

What is happening with respect to immigration issues in your community, and how is this affecting wage rates? Are fewer immigrants available in the labor pool because of enforcement actions?

Surveillance

Analyze whether you want to have a camera system and an alarm system at your franchise.

Many business owners, and employees, resist the idea of having an on-premise camera security system, viewing it with suspicion and a threat to privacy.

> ***Secret #38:*** *Most employees end up appreciating a camera system, particularly one that can be viewed over the internet.*

Here is the reason. Having the ability to view the operations remotely enables the franchisee to see things that would otherwise be hidden or unknown. Oftentimes, some employees seem great when they are being directly supervised by the owner, but may goof off (or worse) when the owner is gone. That can cause huge morale problems among the employees, because the good employees are typically unwilling to "rat" on the employee who is deceiving the owner. A camera system solves that.

Story: We thought Alan was a great employee. He was fast, friendly, hard-working, and ambitious every time we were there. When we weren't there, things didn't get done as quickly, if at all, and of course, there was lots of finger-pointing. We installed a camera system, and observed that as soon as we left, he would grab a giant drink, go to our desk, and play video games. We fired him.

A camera system also protects employees from unreasonable, and even threatening, customers. A robber or intruder will be far less likely to commit mischief if they know that a camera system is recording their every move. Even obnoxious customers (no, the customer is NOT always right) will be less likely to exhibit inappropriate behavior if they know they are being recorded.

Besides, it's fun to call the store when you see something minor that needs correcting, and let the employees know you are watching. Then, they don't really know when you are watching and when you're not, so they think they are being observed all the time.

Finally, having a camera system is something of a deterrent to false Workers Comp claims. If most actions are being recorded, an employee is less likely to claim a "slip and fall".

What kind of camera system should you get?

> ***Secret #39:*** *Camera security systems, which can be viewed over the web, are now amazingly inexpensive – if you know where to look.*

Here's a good distributor for medium quality security systems:

Security Cameras Direct: http://securitycamerasdirect.com/

Their customer service has been excellent, and their products, while not at the top end, are adequate and fairly priced. For smaller businesses, here is what you need to do:

Determine how many cameras you need to cover your location. You'll want to look at your cash register, customer service areas, doors, stocking areas, etc. Buy the number and type of cameras you need.

Buy an internet-ready DVR with enough channels to handle the number of cameras you need, i.e. 4 channels, 8 channels, or 16 channels. Get as much storage capacity as you can afford. Ship the DVR and cameras to your location.

Install the system. Think about where you want to locate the DVR: it needs to be handy to a power supply and your internet router, but you don't want it too accessible. You want to make it difficult for a thief or an employee to remove, disconnect, or damage the equipment. If you're handy, stringing the cable to the cameras is not that hard. If you're techno-phobic, here's a great tip for finding an inexpensive resource who can install the system: find a geek who serves individuals and small businesses. You don't need to go to a security system company. They will want to charge you a lot for equipment, for installation, and for monthly monitoring. How do you find a geek? Google "computer service small business [your county]" and a number of choices will pop up. Call a number of providers until you find someone you like.

View your cameras over the internet!

Step 6 - Marketing/Advertising

National Marketing funds

It is important that you thoroughly understand whether the franchise you are considering requires the collection of National Marketing funds. This is a percentage of your sales that is over and above the royalty that you will pay. Here are the questions you need to find out from the franchisor:

Are National Marketing funds currently collected? If not, is there a provision in the Franchise Agreement that would enable the collection of these funds in the future?

If so, be sure to thoroughly understand these clauses.

How much money is being collected for this National Marketing? What is the percentage being collected from individual franchises, and how often has this changed in the last five years? What is the process for changing the amount being collected: do all existing franchises vote, or is there a ceiling that might enable the franchisor to unilaterally change the rate?

Who gets the money? This is extremely important, and the answer is not obvious! Does the franchisor get the money? Or does a separate organization get the funds? In the Subway system, the funds are collected by the franchisor, but are turned over to a Trust Fund that is independently (more or less) managed.

Who determines how the funds are being spent? Is it the franchisor only; is it a committee, which has representation from the franchisee community? How independent is this body from the franchisor?

What has been the history of spending of the funds? Has the franchisee community been satisfied overall with the results and the allocation of funds? Has there been turnover in the management team that spends the funds?

How is the money being spent? On what media: TV, Radio, direct mail, internet advertising, social media, etc. What is the strategic advertising plan?

> **Secret #40:** *Check for legal action with respect to the collection and spending of marketing funds. This has been an area of extreme acrimony for many franchise systems.*

What is the strategic vision for the distribution of these funds? How is the organization taking advantage of the proliferation of the internet to communicate its message? If there have been enough funds in the past for running a lot of TV and radio, how is the organization addressing the dilution of the influence of mainstream media?

Is a percentage of the National Marketing fund allocated back to local or regional advertising organizations? If so, how much is allocated back for local spending? On what basis: percentage collected, # of stores, etc.?

Local area funds

If marketing funds are collected by the franchisor and allocated for spending in a local area, you need to answer the following questions:

Who gets the local area funds? Is it an independent advertising agency? Is it a committee of franchisees?

How are the decisions made about how the funds are spent?

How satisfied and/or involved are the local franchisees in how the local advertising money is spent?

What is the process that governs which franchisees get decision-making capability about how the local funds are spent? How much influence does the franchisor have on how the money is spent?

> ***Secret #41:*** *If an individual owns multiple franchises in a territory, or if a close group of franchisees owns many of the franchises, that person or group may be able to direct the funds to benefit their stores the most.*

Store/Business marketing

Here's the most important secret about spending additional money for advertising your business:

> ***Secret #42:*** *It doesn't matter how much money the franchisor collects for advertising: every franchise store MUST spend some additional money on local advertising and promotion.*

Many franchisees make the fatal assumption that they can just open their doors and wait for business to be driven into their stores. Even if you have a popular franchise in a great location, you will get better results if you reach out to your local community.

> ***Secret #43:*** *Sometimes no amount of local store marketing can turn around the results of a poor location.*

If you are looking at a low-volume store, don't be fooled by thinking you can single-handedly stimulate a dramatic turnaround in sales volume by doing lots of advertising.

Next, you must thoroughly understand the rules for local advertising. Here are some questions to ask:

- What is the franchisor's training for local advertising? Do other franchisees consider the training very effective?

- What are the guidelines and rules for doing local advertising? Does the franchisor provide a set of templates that the franchisee is free to use? Or does the franchisor, or some other decision-maker, have to approve every single marketing effort in writing? Is so, how responsive is the franchisor to requests?

- Does the franchisor have a recommendation for how much the franchisee should be spending on local store marketing? Have you built these numbers into your business plan?

- How responsive has the franchisor been to the franchisee needs for local marketing?

- Can you create your own website? How much of the website content can/does the franchisor control? What about email marketing?

Here are some ideas for local store marketing that we have found that work:

- Write a series of articles about your business for local publications.

- Collect email addresses of your existing customers, for instance, by offering a "fish bowl" for customers. Send them periodic information or "ethical bribes" to consume your product or service more often. Use an inexpensive emailing service like Constant Contact (www.constantcontact.com).

- Make charitable contributions to local organizations you support

- Send periodic flyers or postcards to surrounding businesses and/or consumers

- If appropriate, join your local Chamber of Commerce

- If appropriate, join a local chapter of BNI (check out http://www.bni.com) or another networking group

- If appropriate, hold free seminars at your business to educate potential customers about the advantages of your business

Secret #44: Make postings on blogs that your prospects are reading, and be sure to provide your contact information in your blog post.

Secret #45: Offer to do testimonials for local businesses that you use that would also reach your potential or existing customers.

Be sure to have your business prominently featured in the testimonial. For instance, let's say you want more local residents as customers, and you observe that there is a popular dry-cleaner that you use in the local area. Offer to write a testimonial that they could post in their store, or in their advertising, or on their website. You are then promoting both their business – and yours!

Customer Service

Good customer service is critical to most franchises. Good customer service leads to word-of-mouth advertising, which is the lowest cost marketing you can do.

You need to understand how much assistance the franchisor is going to provide to ensure your franchise can deliver good customer service.

Here are questions to ask the franchisor:

- What customer-service training courses does the franchisor provide? Are there separate courses for the franchisees, for managers, and for employees?

- How are the courses delivered: at the franchisor location, by the Area Developer, or online? When and how often are the courses delivered?

- In the opinion of other franchisees, what is the quality of the training? Can individuals in the business track their training separately?

- Is the franchisor making constant changes and updates to the training materials? When the franchisor makes changes to its processes or procedures, how diligent are they about communicating and training the franchisee community on these changes?

- If appropriate to the franchise you are considering, is the training offered in English only, or is it also offered in other languages, especially Spanish?

Here are other questions you need to ask to make sure that good Customer Service is a part of your business:

- What other Customer Service training should I implement that is not offered by the franchisor? An example might be a course in basic computer usage offered to ESL employees.

- How much time, effort, and money should I spend on formal Customer Service training? Be sure to add this as a line item in your Business Plan.

Action: Articulate a Customer Service Plan that incorporates both franchisor-provided Customer Service training and independent initiatives.

Step 7 - Business Plan

In this section, I am not going to discuss the specifics of putting together a comprehensive business plan. There are some fine organizations and consultants that can help you accomplish this, and there is some excellent software available as well. I recommend that any business owner create a Business Plan on at least an annual basis, and compare their performance to their Business Plan.

Instead, I will focus on some of the secrets to consider when putting a business plan in place, especially when creating a business plan for a franchise acquisition.

Labor Schedule

Many brokers and franchisors will insinuate a certain labor percentage as being normal for the business. It is natural for the prospective franchisee to believe that they could do better, maybe substantially better, than normal. Here's a secret that will help you make certain that your labor estimates are realistic.

> **Secret #46:** Do not plan labor costs as a percentage. Calculate your planned labor expense by creating a sample schedule.

By creating a sample schedule, this means putting in the number and type of employees you will need each hour, from pre-opening until post-close for each day the business is open. Attach a labor rate to each type of employee, and you will have the daily and weekly gross labor cost. Be sure to add employer taxes plus workers comp and payroll preparation fees to arrive at the true labor cost.

Note: This is especially important if you are buying a franchise that is underperforming or is being run by an owner who is spending a lot of time in the business. For example, the owner-operator may be closing the business alone at night, but you may not be able to do this, and you would want the business to be closed by two employees. You will only be able to articulate the real costs of this change by creating a mock schedule.

Lease

We articulated many of the details of a lease that will need to be examined in the Location section of this book. For Business Plan purposes, step back and take a big picture look at your lease situation.

Here are the big questions:

Is the lease cost reasonable, as a percent of existing sales? For instance, in the restaurant industry, a well-established rule of thumb is that the lease shouldn't be more than 2 days' sales. Be sure to consult with an industry expert before you buy the business. Do NOT overpay on your lease: this should be a DEAL-KILLER.

Action: Be sure to include the CAM (Common Area Maintenance) charges in your Business Plan, and be sure to understand how they are calculated.

Is the lease term appropriate to your plan for the business? Just because there may only be a short time left on the existing term doesn't make it a bad deal, but it is more dangerous. What you don't want is to pay $250,000 for a business with 18 months left on the lease, and then have the landlord back you into a corner upon lease renewal if you really want to stay. On the other hand, if rates are trending down, this could work in your favor. And a short remaining term may give you the opportunity to re-locate the business to a more favorable location if you feel the location is less than ideal. If there is only a short time left, you can use that as leverage to reduce the price for the business. On the other hand, if you are quite certain that you will want to stay in the same location, you MUST negotiate either a new lease with the landlord, or at least an option to renew for the term you would like.

What is the assignment clause? If you are buying a franchise business, it is ideal if the franchisor is the primary tenant, and they can sublease to any qualified franchisee of the system. At least attempt to negotiate a clause that allows the franchisee to assign the lease to any other fully qualified franchisee upon written notice to the landlord.

> **Secret #47:** Hire an independent consultant to negotiate your lease.

If you do need to lease commercial property as part of your business, I highly recommend that YOU PAY an independent professional to negotiate your lease for you. Google "commercial lease consultant" or have discussions with local real estate attorneys or commercial real estate brokers.

> **Secret #48:** Offer to pay a good commercial real estate broker around 2% of your anticipated total lease payment UP FRONT in order to act as your dedicated consultant.

This will insure that your broker is working diligently on your behalf, and has motivation to help you get the best deal. You might even require that the broker NOT participate in the commission split for a successful deal, or alternatively, refund your payment if they do receive a commission. Be patient, and turn down a lot of offers, and develop at least 3-4 alternative locations every time your lease comes up for renewal.

Financing

As we've advised earlier in this book, here's a big secret:

> **Secret #49:** Don't get institutional (bank or other formal company) financing for your first franchise.

If you really want that $150,000 franchise, and you don't have the cash, my strong advice is to pass on that opportunity. There are many franchises that require a far lower investment in order to get started. Build your cash up with those, and then buy the larger deal when you have the cash.

The only exception to financing your first franchise is if you can get seller financing at extremely favorable terms. This might include no payments for the first year, followed by interest only payments for the next 2-5 years, followed by a balloon or better yet, fully amortizing payments over a 5-10 year timeframe.

Create a Mastermind Team

The classic book "Think and Grow Rich" by Napoleon Hill articulated a concept called a MasterMind group, where each member has some skill that supports the other members.

> **Action: form a Mastermind group for your business.**

What do I mean by Mastermind Group? At first this might include an independent business broker (pay them up front for their advice), a good accountant, a business attorney, and a business coach or mentor.

After you acquire the franchise, be sure to add other franchisees, join local Chambers of Commerce, and BNI (go to www.BNI.com).

Finally, check out the resources available to you at the SBA (www.sba.gov), SCORE (Service Corps of Retired Executives at www.score.org), and your local SBDC (Small Business Development Center), an arm of the SBA.

Having a team around you that supports you in your effort and helping you reach your goal is a very effective way that successful franchisees use to excel.

Selling the Business

Always keep in mind what it would take to sell the business. With every major decision you make, you should always ask: "How would this decision impact my ability to sell the business?"

Remember: Circumstances change! Your spouse or significant other might get an awesome job in another country, you or your spouse or your parents may develop health issues that require your full time attention, you may get sick of the business, you may decide you want to take off and go sailing!

Always ask: Am I making decisions that make it easier or harder to find a buyer?

The 3 Deadly Traps

Deadly Trap #1: "Franchises are safe"

"Franchises are much safer investments than independent businesses."

Have you ever heard this, or one of its derivatives?

Don't believe it!

Here's why it's a trap.

The excited first-time franchisee convinces himself or herself that a certain franchise is a great opportunity, and furthermore, the prospective franchisee has found a location that is PERFECT for the franchise. The franchisor concurs, the Area Developer slaps him on the back and tells him it's a no-brainer, the real estate broker (being paid by the landlord) congratulates him on his genius. Before he knows it, he spends $400,000, most of it borrowed from his IRA and institutional lenders to build out the location.

Next, the doors open, and customers stay away in droves. The first-time franchisee (who did not read my book) finds himself working 15 hours a day in the business, and still writing checks to the business at the end of the month.

After 3 years, during which time he's lost the remainder of his retirement funds, he is delighted to sell the business to another franchisee for $100,000. He just lost $300,000 or more, plus the opportunity cost because he could have had a job. Ouch!

The $100,000 franchisee works less, and makes a little more money, but it's still not very profitable, so he sells it 2 years later for $50,000 to a savvy investor (who has read my book). She makes good money.

Does that sound safe???

The franchisor points and says "Only 3% of our locations have ever failed! We're geniuses at choosing locations! Trust us." They don't HAVE to disclose that some poor investors lost $350,000 each on a large percentage of their franchise locations.

This is the deadly trap. You're not going to fall for that one, because you have now read this book!

Deadly Trap #2: "The Ideal Location"

"We'll help you select an ideal location."

Have you heard this one?

Whenever you hear this one, here is the translation:

"We'll help you select the next available location."

Think about it. Who is more strongly motivated to get a location open: the franchisor or the franchisee? More importantly, how much money is the franchisor putting up to get the location open? Answer: $0.00

After investing $0.00 in the location, when does the franchisor start making pure profit from that location? Answer: the minute the store sells $1.00 worth of product.

When do you, the franchisee, start making money from your location? You start making money after you have paid the following expenses:

- The franchisor's initial franchise fee.

- The contractor hired to construct your tenant improvements

- The "Security Deposit" for your lease

- The 1st and last month's rent

- The local and state governments for permits, licenses, entitlements, etc.

- The franchisor's royalty and marketing fees

- The vendors who supply your materials

- The employees, and the additional taxes, workers comp, disability, paid sick leave

- The landlord's lease payments

- The landlord's CAM charges

- The electricity, water, garbage, security, and phone bills
- The equipment repair guy
- The insurance agent for General Liability insurance
- The bank who processes your credit card charges
- Your accountant who tells you how much money you lost
- Other vendors who magically appear just in case you have a little money left in your bank account at the end of the month

*So who has the stronger motivation to get **any** location open?* Answer: the franchisor.

Look, they're not going to let you go into a location that is obviously a loser, but they know that any SALES you generate will benefit them immediately. Therefore, they are going to err on the side of just getting any half-way decent location open.

You need to be completely aware of this dangerous trap!

Deadly Trap #3: "Business in a Box"

"All you have to do is just execute."

How many times have you heard this?

The franchisor says: "The beauty of our franchise is that we have mastered the success formula!! And for only $XXX,XXX.XX, we'll train you in our secret processes. All you have to do is follow the recipe and VOILA! Instant riches and the American Dream are yours!"

Here's the translation:

"All you have to do is work 15 hours per day, 7 days per week, for 18 months or until you have a psychotic break, whichever comes first. Then MAYBE, and ONLY IF you have made all the right decisions, you can write yourself a check for a portion of what you could have been earning in that unsatisfying job you now have."

That's the deadliest trap of them all.

Conclusion

My purpose in writing this book is to equip you with real-world knowledge about how the franchise world is structured. This is my attempt to give you knowledge that is frequently hidden, that usually takes years to acquire, and that could save you (or make you) thousands of dollars. This is knowledge that will empower you to make the right decision for your future.

Much of the franchise industry is geared toward encouraging would-be entrepreneurs to become franchisees. For some, this is a perfect route, and can be deeply satisfying and rewarding.

For others, becoming a franchisee would be an enormous and devastating mistake.

Remember, there are many ways to own your business: you could buy a franchise, you could buy an existing independent business, you could start your own independent business either in a physical location or online, or you could invest in real estate or the stock market. Making the right choice depends on your strengths, desires, and resources. I am honored to help you in your decision-making process.

Appendix 1 - The 49 Secrets

Step 1 - Suitability

Secret #1: To be a successful restaurant franchisee, you need to "follow the recipe". You cannot innovate, create new menu items, revise the décor, and most likely not even dictate the hours the restaurant is open for business.

Secret #2: Most franchises are essentially "buying a job" with an average income range of $30,000 - $60,000 per year if 1) there is no debt; and 2) the franchisee works long hours in the business.

Secret #3: If flipping businesses for profit is your goal, DO NOT BECOME A FRANCHISEE!

Secret #4: To maximize your likelihood of being successful, for your first franchise, pay ALL CASH ONLY!

Secret #5: Answer this question: "Would I (we) like to take a week-long vacation on a remote island with these franchisees?"

Secret #6: A rapidly growing franchise might mean that the franchisor is sacrificing store profitability by putting locations too close together.

Secret #7: The Area Developer is your "Boss".

Secret #8: The Area Developer often gets a higher percentage of your revenue if they sell you a new location than if you buy an existing location. Therefore, they have a strong economic incentive to persuade you to build a new location.

Secret #9: Owning a franchise is far more subject to political forces than owning an independent business.

Step 2 - Trends

Secret #10: See if you can get local market research for free from the provider, or the franchisor, or from the franchisee association, or from an acquaintance at an ad agency serving customers in this area.

Secret #11: Take a knowledgeable Commercial Real Estate broker to lunch. Probe him or her on the general perception of the franchise, and ask the broker their opinion on the concept. What you learn may surprise you!

Secret #12: Wander around the neighborhood where you are most likely to acquire your business. How many "Help Wanted" signs do you see in the types of establishments that are employing your prospective employees?

Step 3 - Location

Secret #13: If you are a first-time franchisee, DO NOT BUY OR BUILD A NEW LOCATION!

Secret #14: The strongest and most fundamental motivation of the franchisor is to get more system-wide sales on which they get paid a royalty. It is not to make franchisees profitable.

Secret #15: If a franchisee is losing money, or sells their franchise and loses their investment, the franchisor does not report this is a failure! In fact, they will report the fact that the location has been successfully operating in that location for x years!

Secret #16: Make sure you know exactly what the process is, if any, for recovering your franchise fee if the franchisor cannot or will not approve a location for you within a specified period of time.

Secret #17: Oftentimes the most profitable locations are the ones you would not suspect.

Secret #18: Be sure to find out if the Seller is employing family, and paying under the table, therefore under-reporting the true cost of labor. Is the spouse doing all the books, are the children working, etc.?

Secret #19: If you plan to work LESS in the business than the current owner does, you obviously need to increase the labor cost. AND, you need to adjust projected sales down, and increase your cost of goods.

Secret #20: Be sure to ask the franchisor what their plans are for requiring an upgrade to the POS system or other technology initiatives, and what their cost estimate is. This can often be a $20,000 investment.

Secret #21: The value of the business, if you ever intend to sell it, depends to a large degree on the lease terms.

Secret #22: Landlords will frequently grant a tenant improvement allowance upon lease renewal.

Secret #23: Most assignments do not allow the original tenant (you) to be released from the obligation to pay the rent even with an assignment.

Secret #24: Thoroughly understand the Franchisor's assignment process BEFORE you agree to buy a franchise, and accept that selling a franchise involves significantly more "friction", ancillary costs, and time, than selling an independent business.

Step 4 - Due Diligence

Secret #25: If there is a lot of litigation listed in the FDD that has occurred or is still pending within the last 2 years, avoid this opportunity.

Secret #26: Note the franchisee obligations from the FDD that surprise you. When you speak with existing and former franchisees, be sure to discuss these specific obligations, and how diligently they are enforced by the franchisor.

Secret #27: Even if you don't have territory protection from the franchisor, examine whether you have protection from outside forces.

Secret #28: Schedule talks with the ex-franchisees: call every single one, up to 50 of them.

Secret #29: Find out hidden information from ex-franchisees. Ask the ex-franchisees who the formal and information leaders are, and ask to borrow past years' copies of FDDs or UFOCs.

Secret #30: Many existing franchisees will shade their answers to your questions to the positive side. Why? Because they may want to sell to you, or they are afraid of retribution by the franchisor or Area Developer if word got back that they were expressing negative sentiments about the business. READ BETWEEN THE LINES!

Secret #31: Don't buy a franchise, any franchise, unless you can make a lot more money than non-franchise competitors.

Step 5 - Employees

Secret #32: Just because your concept requires low-paid employees, you cannot assume that it will be easy to find such employees.

Secret #33: Right now, many QSR's are hurting for employees because of the enormous competition from the coffee stores, like Starbucks.

Secret #34: During those inevitable times when you lose key employees, YOU will be filling in, GUARANTEED.

Secret #35: I don't know of ANY franchises that can be run successfully with absentee owners.

Secret #36: If you are buying your first franchise, you MUST plan on working the business full-time (50-70 hours per week) for the first year.

Secret #37: It is almost impossible to hire reliable, hard-working workers in affluent communities, even at high wages.

Secret #38: Most employees end up appreciating a camera system, particularly one that can be viewed over the internet.

Secret #39: Camera security systems, which can be viewed over the web, are now amazingly inexpensive – if you know where to look.

Step 6 - Marketing/Advertising

Secret #40: Check for legal action with respect to the collection and spending of marketing funds. This has been an area of extreme acrimony for many franchise systems.

Secret #41: If an individual owns multiple franchises in a territory, or if a close group of franchisees owns many of the franchises, that person or group may be able to direct the group marketing funds to benefit their stores the most.

Secret #42: It doesn't matter how much money the franchisor collects for advertising: every franchise store MUST spend some additional money on local advertising and promotion.

Secret #43: Sometimes no amount of local store marketing can turn around the results of a poor location.

Secret #44: Make postings on blogs that your prospects are reading, and be sure to provide your contact information in your blog post.

Secret #45: Offer to do testimonials for local businesses that you use that would also reach your potential or existing customers.

Step 7 - Business Plan

Secret #46: Do not plan labor costs as a percentage. Calculate your planned labor expense by creating a sample schedule.

Secret #47: Prepay a commercial real estate broker to act as an independent consultant to negotiate your lease.

Secret #48: Offer to pay a good commercial real estate broker around 2% of your anticipated total lease payment UP FRONT in order to act as your dedicated consultant.

Secret #49: Don't get institutional (bank or other formal company) financing for your first franchise.

Resources

Kolbe test
http://www.kolbe.com

Bureau of Labor Statistics
http://www.bls.gov/

Census data
http://www.census.gov/

Sandelman and Associates
http://www.sandelman.com/

Security Cameras Direct
http://www.securitycamerasdirect.com/

Constant Contact
http://www.constantcontact.com

BNI
http://www.bni.com

Small Business Administration (SBA)
http:// www.sba.gov

Service Corps of Retired Executives (SCORE)
http://www.score.org

Small Business Development Center (SBDC)
Check local listings

About the Author

In 2001, Mark conducted research on hundreds of franchise opportunities, and chose to acquire 3 franchise locations of a highly rated franchise in the San Francisco Bay Area. Mark participated very actively in the franchisee community, including being elected to the Board of Directors of the regional Franchisee Advertising Fund, and he was also Chairperson of the Northern California Materials Council. After selling his franchises, he wrote "7 Steps ..." to help prospective franchisees make good franchise investment decisions.

Prior to his franchise ownership, Mark spent 20+ years in Silicon Valley in roles including finance, contract management, sales, marketing, and CEO, starting with ROLM/IBM and including several software design firms. Mark earned an MBA from the University of Virginia's Darden School, and an undergraduate degree from Davidson College, North Carolina.

Mark can be reached at mark@ datagroup.com.